Le
Noct

MW00929082

Sy Barlowe

DOVER PUBLICATIONS, INC.
Mineola, New York

Bibliographical Note

Learning About Nocturnal Creatures is a new work,
first published by Dover Publications, Inc., in 2020.

International Standard Book Number
ISBN-13: 978-0-486-84457-2
ISBN-10: 0-486-84457-9

Manufactured in the United States by Phoenix Color
84457901   2020
www.doverpublications.com

Introduction

While we are asleep, creatures of the night are busy hunting, feeding, and playing. To help guide them through the dark, these animals have developed some very special ways to use their senses of sight, hearing, and smell. From the swooping "sonar"-equipped bat to the clever fox and the muffled wings of the owl, these animals fill the night with silent activity. Add each sticker to the appropriate page and find out more about these fascinating animals.

Long-tailed Weasel

Found throughout almost the entire United States, this small but fierce killer attacks prey much larger than itself, such as rabbits, squirrels, and poultry. Although farmers consider the 16-inch-long animal a pest, the weasel also helps them by killing harmful rodents that destroy crops. Weasels living in the north change the color of their coats to white in the winter, except for the tip of the tail, which remains black.

Raccoon

Related to the pandas of Asia, raccoons have a broad black stripe across the eyes. They will eat almost anything—fruits, vegetables, small mammals, birds, and insects. Feeding at streams and ponds, they appear to be "washing" their food, but they are actually using the water to soften their food with their sensitive paws. In the suburbs, raccoons pry open the lids of garbage cans to search for food.

Striped Skunk

With its bold coat of black and white, the skunk doesn't need protective coloring to defend itself. Little wonder! It is capable of spraying a foul-smelling scent up to 15 feet, so predators leave this animal alone. Although nocturnal, the skunk may be seen during the day feeding mostly on insects, fruit, and berries. It also preys on mice and birds.

Coyote

From sharp barks to long howls, the song of the coyote remains on the western prairies as a reminder of the American Old West. Now found in some eastern states as well, coyotes will eat almost anything, including an occasional sheep or chicken. They also eat mice and other crop destroyers. The coyote is one of the fastest mammals in North America, running at speeds of up to 40 miles per hour.

1

2

3

4

5

6

AFTER ALL THE STICKERS HAVE BEEN PLACED IN THE CORRECT SPACES,
PLEASE GENTLY REMOVE AND DISCARD THESE TWO PAGES.

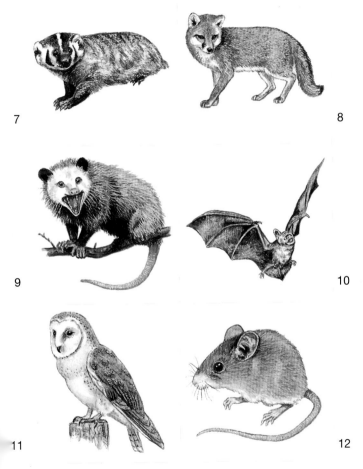

7

8

9

10

11

12

AFTER ALL THE STICKERS HAVE BEEN PLACED IN THE CORRECT SPACES,
PLEASE GENTLY REMOVE AND DISCARD THESE TWO PAGES.   84457-9

White-tailed Deer

The white-tailed deer is the most hunted big game in the United States. When frightened, it speeds away and raises its tail, white on the underside, which flashes a warning to its fawn and other deer. Only the male has antlers, and these appear in their third year. The deer feeds on acorns, leaves, and fruit, browsing on twigs and buds in the winter.

Bobcat

Also known as the wildcat, this bold hunter preys on hares, ground squirrels, rodents, and even bats. It has been known to attack animals much larger than itself. Found in most of North America, it is named for its short, or "bobbed," tail, and is a smaller version of the Canada lynx. When cornered, the bobcat is famous for its ferocity in defending itself.

Badger

This fierce, flat-bodied, digging mammal is found in the West, on the prairies and deserts of the United States. Helped by its long front claws, it hunts a wide variety of small burrowing animals, birds, and insects. If threatened, the badger digs into the soft sand with amazing speed. Bad-tempered, this nocturnal hunter is a constant threat to other shy creatures of the night.

Gray Fox

A fox that climbs trees? Unlike other foxes, the gray fox is an excellent tree climber and will climb to escape danger or hunt for prey. Smaller and more shy than the red fox, it feeds on small mammals, insects, fruits, and grains. Common throughout the eastern and southwestern United States, the gray fox makes its home in caves, crevices, hollow logs, or on rock ledges.

Opossum

Opossums are the only marsupial animals found in North America. (A marsupial is a mammal that carries its young in its pouch.) The mother takes her babies wherever she goes, letting them ride on her back after they have matured enough to come out of the pouch. Opossums eat a diet of small animals, birds' eggs, and fruit. When threatened, they will collapse and play dead, causing their attacker to leave.

Brown Myotis Bat

One of the only mammals that can fly, the brown myotis, or little brown bat, feeds at night on flying insects. Bats send out high-pitched sounds and listen for the echo to find out an object's exact location. They may eat hundreds of insects each night, traveling a distance of up to 50 miles. During the day, they roost in caves, hollow trees, and barns.

Barn Owl

This strange-looking bird is also known as the monkey-faced owl and ghost owl. With its superb hearing and nearly perfect eyesight (even in the dark), the barn owl is a deadly predator of mice and rats. During its nightly hunt for food, the owl relies on its flight feathers to hush its own noise and uses its tufted ears to listen for any signs of danger.

House Mouse

Originally found in Asia, this 6- or 7-inch mouse (including a 3- or 4-inch tail) came to America on the ships of early explorers. Although it prefers living in buildings, this gray mouse can also live outdoors in fields, where it will build a nest made of feathers and paper. Living near people, the house mouse is considered a very destructive pest that can carry many diseases.